MIX
Papier aus verantwortungsvollen Quellen
Paper from responsible sources
FSC® C105338

Marina Stoll

Risk management and management control systems

Similarities and differences

Anchor Academic Publishing

Stoll, Marina: **Risk management and management control systems. Similarities and differences**, Hamburg, Anchor Academic Publishing 2016

Buch-ISBN: 978-3-96067-031-5
PDF-eBook-ISBN: 978-3-96067-531-0
Druck/Herstellung: Anchor Academic Publishing, Hamburg, 2016

Bibliografische Information der Deutschen Nationalbibliothek:
Die Deutsche Nationalbibliothek verzeichnet diese Publikation in der Deutschen Nationalbibliografie; detaillierte bibliografische Daten sind im Internet über http://dnb.d-nb.de abrufbar.

Bibliographical Information of the German National Library:
The German National Library lists this publication in the German National Bibliography. Detailed bibliographic data can be found at: http://dnb.d-nb.de

All rights reserved. This publication may not be reproduced, stored in a retrieval system or transmitted, in any form or by any means, electronic, mechanical, photocopying, recording or otherwise, without the prior permission of the publishers.

Das Werk einschließlich aller seiner Teile ist urheberrechtlich geschützt. Jede Verwertung außerhalb der Grenzen des Urheberrechtsgesetzes ist ohne Zustimmung des Verlages unzulässig und strafbar. Dies gilt insbesondere für Vervielfältigungen, Übersetzungen, Mikroverfilmungen und die Einspeicherung und Bearbeitung in elektronischen Systemen.

Die Wiedergabe von Gebrauchsnamen, Handelsnamen, Warenbezeichnungen usw. in diesem Werk berechtigt auch ohne besondere Kennzeichnung nicht zu der Annahme, dass solche Namen im Sinne der Warenzeichen- und Markenschutz-Gesetzgebung als frei zu betrachten wären und daher von jedermann benutzt werden dürften.

Die Informationen in diesem Werk wurden mit Sorgfalt erarbeitet. Dennoch können Fehler nicht vollständig ausgeschlossen werden und die Diplomica Verlag GmbH, die Autoren oder Übersetzer übernehmen keine juristische Verantwortung oder irgendeine Haftung für evtl. verbliebene fehlerhafte Angaben und deren Folgen.

Alle Rechte vorbehalten

© Anchor Academic Publishing, Imprint der Diplomica Verlag GmbH
Hermannstal 119k, 22119 Hamburg
http://www.diplomica-verlag.de, Hamburg 2016
Printed in Germany

Table of contents

List of figures and tables II
List of abbreviations III
1. Introduction 1
2. Theoretical background 2
    2.1. Risk management 2
        2.1.1. Risk definition and classification 2
        2.1.2. Risk management definition, objectives and tasks 3
        2.1.3. Risk management process 4
    2.2. Management control systems 7
        2.2.1. Definition and purposes 7
        2.2.2. Different frameworks and understandings 8
3. **Legal framework and the relation between risk management and management control systems** 12
    3.1. Committee of Sponsoring Organizations of the Treadway Commission 13
    3.2. Corporate governance and the Sarbanes-Oxley Act of 2002 14
    3.3. The comparison of risk management and management control systems 14
        3.3.1. The main similarities 15
            3.3.1.1. Objectives 15
            3.3.1.2. Strategies 15
            3.3.1.3. Processes 15
            3.3.1.4. Balanced scorecards and balanced chance- and risk-cards 16
        3.3.2. The main differences 17
            3.3.2.1. Objectives 17
            3.3.2.2. Processes 18
        3.3.3. Summarizing table 18
4. Summary and conclusion 20
List of references 21

List of figures and tables

Figures

Figure 1: Exemplary risk categorization 3
Figure 2: The CIMA risk management cycle 4
Figure 3: Risk Heat Map 6
Figure 4: Risk treatment strategies 6
Figure 5: The performance management systems (PMSs) framework 11
Figure 6: Management control systems package 12
Figure 7: IC – Integrated Framework 13
Figure 8: ERM – Integrated Framework 13

Tables

Table 1: Similarities and differences of RM and MCSs – A summary 18/19

List of abbreviations

BCR(-card)	Balanced chance- and risk(-card)
BSC	Balanced scorecard
CFaR	Cash-flow-at-risk
CG	Corporate governance
CIMA	Chartered Institute of Management Accountants
COSO	Committee of Sponsoring Organizations of the Treadway Commission
ERM	Enterprise risk management
EVA	Economic value added
FRCS	Financial results control system
HR	Human resources
IC	Internal control
IRM	Institute of Risk Management
KPMG	Klynveld, Peat, Marwick, Goerdeler (named after the founders)
MC	Management control
MCS	Management control system
PMS	Performance management system
RM	Risk management
ROI	Return on investment
SOA/SOX	Sarbanes-Oxley Act
VaR	Value-at-risk

1. Introduction

The objective of every for-profit organization is to earn profit, to secure its existence and to meet stakeholders' expectations, but every company is confronted with certain risks. Some are easy to handle, others are existence-threatening. This makes it difficult to achieve these objectives. The accumulation of global economic crises, frauds, and financial scandals, but also terrorist attacks and failures in large computer systems, shows that businesses are faced with greater challenges than before and how important it is to manage risks. Hence, companies have to implement risk management systems and processes to identify, assess and treat risks, and so to create transparency over the risk situation and to plan for the future. Many of these risks and problems are externally given, but some also result from the misconduct of a company's managers and employees. However, owners and managers of a business are not always the same, and growing businesses need to employ more and more people to bring the company to success, but employees do not always behave in the company's aim – sometimes intended, sometimes unintended (this subject is often described through the so called *principal agent theory*[1]). This leads to the need of systems that help to control employees and managers and ensure that they behave in the firm's sense. These systems are called *management control systems*.

But what is more effective and efficient in supporting the company to reach its goals, risk management or management control systems? There is a research gap concerning this question. Thus, the resulting questions are the following ones: What exactly is risk management? What exactly is a management control system? Which are the similarities and differences of both? Is it perhaps possible to combine both to reach a kind of perfect control system for businesses? This paper is intended to answer these questions.

It is structured into four sections as follows. Section 1 gives a short introduction to the subject, states the research questions and contains the outline of this paper. Section 2 introduces the theoretical background of both, risk management and management control systems, i.e. definitions, processes and different understandings are introduced. Section 3 can be seen as the core of the paper, because it focuses on the legal framework and the relation between risk management and management control systems. It first describes issues concerning rules and legislations, then compares risk management and management control systems directly. Section 4 summarizes all key findings and answers to the questions above and shows areas for future research.

---

[1] For a brief description of the principal agent theory see: Tirole, 2001, pp. 1-2.

2. Theoretical background

This chapter contains the theoretical background of the paper and focuses on the basic theory of risk management and management control systems. It first gives an introduction to the terms of risk and risk management and describes the risk management process. Then it provides a closer look at management control systems, i.e. definitions, purposes, and different understandings.

2.1. Risk management

2.1.1. Risk definition and classification

The starting point for handling risks in a company is a clear definition of risk, and defining risks is fundamentally for an effective risk management practice which I will refer to in the next subchapter.

The origin of the term *risk* is presumably the Italian word *risco* which can be translated with *danger* or *responsibility*. Risk definitions vary widely in literature, and so no generally accepted definition has emerged, either in theory or in practice. Nevertheless, risk is a common word which always has something to do with uncertainty and events and their consequences in the future. Some define risks as "potential events that could influence the achievement of the organization's objectives" (Doody, 2009, p. 17), others say "a risk is the effect of uncertainty on objectives" (Meyer et al., 2011, p. 2). A common definition describes risk as the possibility of deviation of a future event from an originally anticipated event (see Cottin & Döhler, 2013, pp. 1-2), thus risk can be both positive and negative deviation. Negative deviation often means risk of damage or loss, and positive deviation means opportunities. In practice risk is usually defined "as the combination of the probability of an event and its consequences" (IRM, 2002, p. 2).

Since we understand now what is meant by risk, we can have a closer look at the different types of risk. One can subdivide these into *internal* and *external risks* (see Diederichs, 2012, pp. 55-57). Internal risks relate to operational business processes and result from entrepreneurial acts. External risks affect the entire company and can be seen as risks from the corporate environment or from society.

Risks can be categorized in many different ways, but according to Diederichs one can classify internal risks as follows in figure 1. The significance of particular types of risk varies from company to company.[2]

---

[2] For further information see: Nevries & Strauß, 2008, pp. 106-111.

Figure 1: *Exemplary risk categorization*[3]

2.1.2. Risk management definition, objectives and tasks

Knowing what the term of risk means, the next step is to clarify what is meant by *risk management* (RM). Such as the term suggests, RM is a system for handling risks. CIMA's *Official Terminology* (2005) describes it as the "process of understanding and managing risks that the entity is inevitably subject to in attempting to achieve its corporate objectives". A more detailed definition says: RM as a part of the company management represents the totality of organizational measures and processes that aims at the identification, assessment, treatment, and monitoring of risks (see Diederichs, 2012, p. 13). First, this description expresses that RM has an accompanying guiding function, and second, it includes the core of RM, namely the RM process which will be considered in the next subchapter.

According to Diederichs (2012, p. 12), the *objectives of a RM system* can be summarized as follows (a long-term orientation is seen):

- livelihood security of the company
- assurance of future success
- market appreciation of the company
- avoidance or reduction of risk costs

To achieve these goals, certain tasks have to be perceived. Derived from the objectives, one can formulate the following *tasks of a RM system*:

- creation of a company-wide risk awareness including the definition of risk and security objectives

---

[3] Source: Diederichs, 2012, p. 56 [translated].

- timely identification of possible risks
- analysis, evaluation and ongoing monitoring of the risk situation of the company
- dealing with risks

In addition, it is important to mention that RM's task is not to keep risks as small as possible or to eliminate them, rather a transparency on the risk situation should be established (see Gleißner, 2011, p. 12). An elimination of risks would not allow any opportunities and would thus lead to entrepreneurial inactivity.

2.1.3. Risk management process

Risk management is not a onetime project, but rather a continuous process that should be run through. The RM process is often represented in the form of a cycle. In economic literature this circulation model consists of three to six stages. For instance in *Fraud risk management* (2009, pp. 19-21), Doody describes six steps included in the risk management cycle and one previous step. The following steps should be taken:

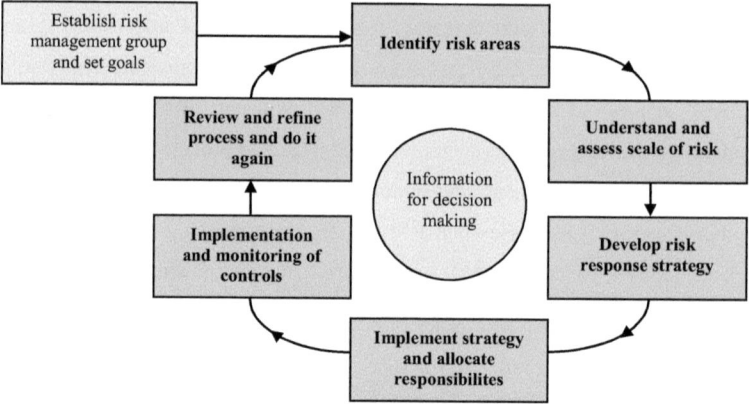

Figure 2: *The CIMA risk management cycle*[4]

Kajüter (2012, p. 114) depicts three main stages that are characterized through *detecting risks at an early stage* (i.e. risk identification, risk assessment, and risk communication), *risk overcoming* (i.e. risk regulation and risk control), and *internal monitoring*. One recognizes that these three steps are less concrete than CIMA's risk management cycle, but more or less they also contain the seven steps above. The literature is a broad consensus that the main phases of the RM process are risk identification, risk assessment,

---

[4] Source: Doody, 2009, p. 19.

risk treatment, and risk monitoring (see Wall, 2003, pp. 457-471), thus in the following the focus is on these four phases which will be described in detail.

The starting point of the RM process is *risk identification* which aims to provide an information basis for the next steps. In this phase that represents the most important one, all significant risks must be fully identified and sorted according to specified categories. If any important risks are not identified, they can lead to serious threats, so there are certain necessary postulates that should be considered: completeness, currency, essentiality and systematics.[5] There can be found several methods and instruments in literature for identifying risks. To capture risks one can use common methods like variance analysis, workshops, brainstorming, interviews, organization plans, balances, check lists, statistics, and visits, but special analysis methods that will be named in the following are more efficient. They have been proved to be particularly useful.[6]

A special method is *Porter's value chain model* which concentrates on the competitive advantages of a company (see Porter, 1999, pp. 63-65). The basic idea consists of identifying relevant activities that the company is more competitive in than others, differentiating them with regard to the end product in primary and secondary activities, and then splitting them into individual activities to identify priority processes. In this way the company can discover which processes are fraught with potential risks and should be considered in more detail. Other methods that work in a similar way are given by *event-driven process chains*, *failure mode and effect analysis*, and *fault tree analysis*.[7] While using all these methods to identify risks one should always try to find a balance between a complete and an economically meaningful risk detection.

In the next step identified risks need to be assessed which leads us to the phase *risk assessment*. The aim is to find out the importance of the individual risks and to classify them accordingly. A simple and common method of assessment is creating a *risk map* or *risk portfolio*, which sets the possible impact of a risk against the corresponding likelihood of occurrence in a graphic.[8] At that, both impacts and likelihoods of occurrence should either be qualitative or quantitative. If a quantitative analysis is not possible, because too little information is available, one could grade risks in high, medium, and low categories. Merchant and Van der Stede present a simple example in a case study and use the following severity scale and likelihood scale:

---

[5] See Diederichs, 2012, pp. 51-52; Kajüter, 2012, pp. 155-156.
[6] See in addition: Romeike, 2005, pp. 17-32.
[7] For further information see: Diederichs, 2012, pp. 62-64; Gleißner, 2011, pp. 66-68.
[8] See Diederichs, 2012, pp. 92-94; Gleißner 2011, pp. 145-147; Kajüter, 2012, pp. 167-168.

Severity	3	3	6	9
	2	2	4	6
	1	1	2	3
		1	2	3
			Likelihood	

Severity scale	Likelihood scale
1 = Not significant	1 = Unlikely to occur in the next 12 months
2 = Significant, but not material	2 = Potential for minor occurrences in the next 12 months
3 = Material	3 = Minor occurrences happening now OR potential for significant occurrences in the next 12 months

Figure 3: *Risk Heat Map*[9]

In a risk map it is readily apparent which risks are significant, because the position of a risk in the map shows its importance and the associated urgency of countermeasures, thus it provides a clear presentation and classification/prioritization of risks. Concerning quantitative and qualitative analyzes, many other methods can be used for assessing risks, e.g. expectation values, distributions, scoring models, scenario technique.[10] Another common risk measure is *value-at-risk* (VaR) that can be defined as the (evaluated in monetary units) maximum loss of a risk position which will not be exceeded with a given probability over a given period.[11] A similar measure is *cash-flow-at-risk* (CFaR), the lowest cash flow which is reached at least with a given probability over a given period (see Diederichs, 2012, p. 117). The biggest problem in this phase is the absence of empirical values, so only estimates can be used and this can lead to faults.

Now that risks are identified, quantified and classified, it is time to think about how to treat them. The assessed risks should be compared to the security objectives of the company and made manageable in the next phase which is named *risk treatment*. In economical literature, mostly four action alternatives or treatment strategies are mentioned.[12] Inspired by this literature, the following frame can be composed:

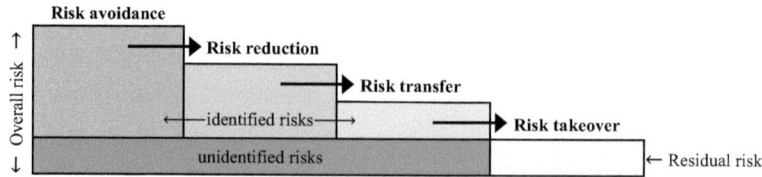

Figure 4: *Risk treatment strategies*[13]

---

[9] Source: Merchant & Van der Stede, 2012, p. 593.
[10] See Frenkel et al., 2000, p. 286; Gleißner, 2011, pp. 111-125.
[11] See Oehler & Unser, 2002, p. 14; Spellmann & Unser, 1998, pp. 261-263.
[12] See Diederichs, 2012, pp. 124-126; Gleißner, 2011, pp. 181-183; Kajüter, 2012, pp. 188-189.
[13] In lean on to: Romeike, 2002, pp. 12-17 [translated].

Risk avoidance reduces the probability of occurrence to zero by giving up certain economic activities (e.g. risky businesses or technologies). This strategy should be applied only in case of existential risks, because profit opportunities will be given up.

Risk reduction reduces the probability of occurrence or/and the impact to acceptable levels by technical or organizational actions (e.g. IT security or outsourcing).

Risk transfer is a strategy for transferring risks to a third party that accepts the harm through contractual arrangements (e.g. statements of insurance).

Risk takeover takes place when a company itself must bear the residual risk, because the other strategies cannot exclude all risks completely. In this case the company needs adequate capital resources and liquidity reserves.

The last step in the RM process is *risk monitoring* which includes reporting and communication of risks. Responsible and decision-making departments should be informed about the risk situation, and the risk report should be integrated into the standard reporting system, so that current developments can be reported. For efficient running a framework needs to be established, i.e. risk responsible people, a reporting calendar, and other important standards have to be chosen.

2.2. Management control systems

2.2.1. Definition and purposes

Trying to find a uniform definition of *management control* (MC) or *management control system* (MCS) is difficult, because books and articles written on management control use different definitions and have different understandings of what is important to mention regarding this subject, but there is also a lot of overlap. The idea of MC and MCSs can be described in the following way: "irrespective of the manager's focus [...] the crucial question is how this manager gets his people to put his visions into practice. So, he needs to think about the appropriate toolbox, i.e. various 'systems' available to influence people's behavior" (Malmi & Schäffer, 2013, p. 42). For that, performance definition is the first thing one should work on, i.e. defining what needs to be done, then measurements should come second, and the third thing to do is providing rewards (see Kerr, 2004, p. 122). MC is the "core function of management" (Merchant & Van der Stede, 2012, p. xii) and many examples of MC failures, e.g. thefts, frauds, unintentional errors, show the importance of having good MCSs. MCs are necessary to reduce the probabilities that employees will do something that is not in the company's interest.

Abernethy and Chua (1996, p. 573) define MCS as "a combination of control mechanisms designed and implemented by management to increase the probability that organizational actors will behave in ways consistent with the objectives of the dominant organizational coalition".

Generalized, one can say that "someone (senior manager/top management team/dominant coalition) is seeking to control the behavior of others (middle management, employees) [and] those systems, rules, practices, values and other activities management put in place in order to direct employee behavior should be called management controls. If these are complete systems [...] then they should be called MCSs" (Brown & Malmi, 2008, pp. 289-290). Budgeting or balanced scorecards can be mentioned as examples for MCSs.

A quite similar device are *performance management systems* (PMSs). Ferreira and Otley (2009, p. 264) define PMSs as "the evolving [...] mechanisms, processes, systems and networks used by organizations for conveying the key objectives [...] elicited by management, for assisting the strategic process and ongoing management through analysis, planning, measurement, control, rewarding, and broadly managing performance, and for supporting and facilitating organizational learning and change."

2.2.2. Different frameworks and understandings

To get a deeper insight into the subject, I next introduce Merchant and Van der Stede's configuration of MCSs (2012), then Ferreira and Otley's PMS framework (2009) and finally I present Brown and Malmi's (2008) MCS package framework.

In *Management Control Systems – Performance Measurement, Evaluation and Incentives* (2012), Merchant and Van der Stede point out that the knowledge of objectives and strategies is very important for MCSs (pp. 7-8). Employees must understand what the company is trying to achieve (*objectives*) and what they are supposed to do for that (*strategies*). Three causes for MC problems are named: *lack of direction*, *motivational problems*, and *personal limitations* (pp. 10-12). They can be removed through informing, motivating, and training. Concretely, Merchant and Van der Stede describe four different management control alternatives which are the following ones (pp. 29-96).

Results control is an indirect form of control, because it empowers employees to do what they think will best lead to the desired results (p. 30). The implementation of results controls consists of *defining performance dimensions*, *measuring performance*, *setting performance targets*, and *providing rewards*, whereby it is important that valued rewards are linked to results employees are able to influence (pp. 33-36). For an effective MC through results controls, certain postulates for measures should be considered: precision, objectivity, timeliness, understandability, cost efficiency (pp. 38-39).

Action control is a direct form of control, because it empowers employees to perform certain actions that are known to be good for the company (p. 81). Action controls have four forms: action accountability, behavioral constraints, preaction reviews, redundancy.

Personnel controls empower employees to "perform the desired tasks satisfactorily on their own", i.e. performing tasks well leads to a kind of self-realization (p. 88).

Finally, *cultural controls* empower employees to "monitor and influence each other's behaviors", i.e. mutual monitoring (p. 90).

While using MCSs, one should always keep in mind that predicting employees' behaviors is difficult, because some of them behave this way and others that way, and so their reactions to the controls can differ a lot. One should always put the costs for MCs against the expected benefits, because MCSs only reduce the probability of bad performance, they do not eliminate it (pp. 12-13).

Merchant and Van der Stede also introduce a special form of results control, namely *financial results control systems* (FRCS). In FRCS, results are defined in terms of accounting measures. FRCSs consist of *financial responsibility centers*, *planning and budgeting systems*, and *incentive contracts* (p. 261). In financial responsibility centers, responsibilities are divided "for a particular set of outputs and/or inputs to an employee in charge of an organizational entity" and are defined in financial terms (p. 262). Four basic types can be differentiated: *investment centers, profit centers, revenue centers, cost centers*. Planning and budgeting systems clarify the company's objectives, strategies and performance targets (p. 306), and finally, incentive systems which mean the provision of rewards are very important, because they motivate employees to reach performance goals (p. 367). Rewards can be both monetary (e.g. performance based salary increases, short-term incentive plans, and long-term incentive plans) and nonmonetary (e.g. praise, recognition, and promotions) (pp. 370-377).

The last subject of Merchant and Van der Stede's configuration are performance measurement issues. For measuring performance, *market measures* and/or *accounting measures* can be used (pp. 414-419). Market measures "reflect changes in stock prices or shareholder returns", and accounting measures are "residual terms (e.g. EVA) or ratio terms (e.g. ROI)" (p. 413). For-profit organizations aim to maximize the firm's value which is a long-term objective, but one big problem of using accounting measures is *myopia*, i.e. short-term orientation (p. 445). Certain remedies can help to solve the myopia problem. Problems also can occur through uncontrollable factors which employees should not be held accountable for. To control the effects of uncontrollable factors a company should purchase insurance, use variance analysis, etc. (pp. 508-511).

Ferreira and Otley concentrate on PMSs in their article *The design and use of performance management systems: An extended framework for analysis* (2009). They worked out an extended framework on the basis of Otley's framework from 1999. This new framework "aims to reflect a shift from the traditional compartmentalized approaches to control in organizations [...] to a broader perspective", and "it also aims to give a managerial emphasis, by integrating various dimensions of managerial activity with the control system" (p. 266). It contains twelve questions which form this *extended PMSs framework* and "can be used to facilitate the description of PMSs design and use in practice, without any prior assumption as to whether the existence or absence of a particular feature is a good or bad thing" (p. 267). In figure 5, these twelve questions are shown in a kind of scheme.

Vision and mission are about determining purposes and objectives of the organization. *Key success factors* are "activities, attributes, competencies, and capabilities that are seen as critical pre-requisites for the success of an organization in its industry at a certain point of time" (p. 268). *Organization structures* are "formed as means of establishing formally the specification of individual roles and tasks to be carried out [...], they entrust and empower individuals to act within their sphere of responsibility" (p. 269). *Strategies and plans* show the long-term direction of the organization and can be seen as "the means of achieving organizational objectives" (p. 270). *Key performance measures* are "the financial or non-financial measures [...] used at different levels in organizations to evaluate success in achieving their objectives, [key success factors], strategies and plans" (p. 271). *Target setting* is about deciding what levels of performance need to be achieved for each of the key performance measures. *Performance evaluation* deals with the question what processes are used for evaluating individuals', groups', and the organization's performance. *Information flows, systems, and networks* can be seen as "the binding agent that keeps the whole system together" (p. 273). *PMSs use* is about different types of using the obtained information and control mechanisms. *PMSs change* explores what kind of changes affect the organization and with it the PMSs design. *Strength and Coherence* consider the links between the components of PMSs, because "there is a need for alignment and coordination between the different components for the whole to deliver efficient and effective outcomes" (p. 275).

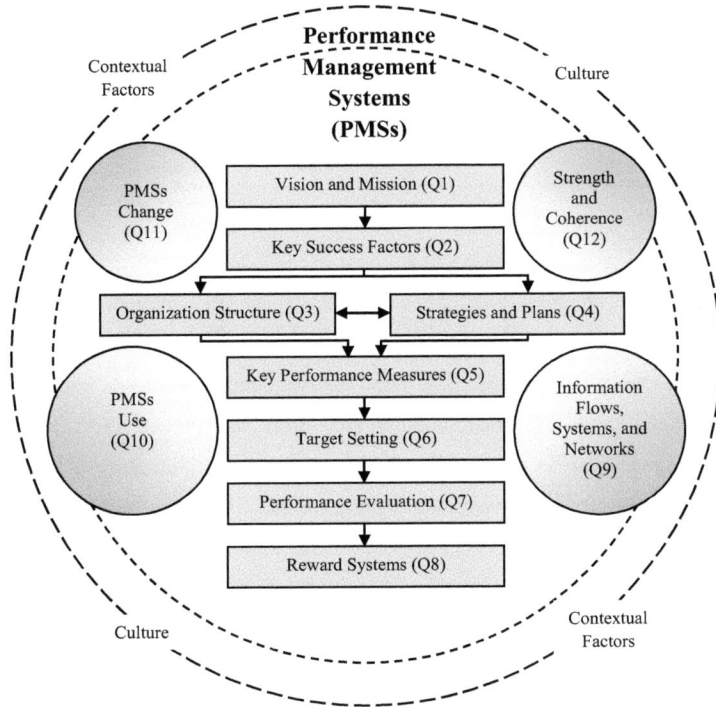

Figure 5: *The performance management systems (PMSs) framework*[14]

The authors conclude: "the PMSs framework provides a tool which [...] describe[s] the structure and use of the 'package' of controls deployed by management [...] to ensure that an organization's strategies and plans are effectively implemented" (p. 277).

In the article *Management control systems as a package – Opportunities, challenges and research directions* (2008), Brown and Malmi present a MCS package framework. They use the term "package", because most organizations use a number of MCSs, and controls should not be defined as a single system, but instead as a package of systems (p. 291). Figure 6 provides this MCS package that consists of five types of controls.

Planning is about setting goals, providing methods and principles to reach them, and controlling these activities, thereby planning can be strategic (some years) or tactical (less than one year) (p. 291).

---

[14] Source: Ferreira & Otley, 2009, p. 268.

Cultural Controls				
Clans		Values		Symbols
Planning		**Cybernetic Controls**		**Reward and Compensation**
Long range planning / Action planning	Budgets	Financial Measurement Systems	Non Financial Measurement Systems / Hybrid Measurement Systems	
Administrative Controls				
Governance Structure		Organization Structure		Policies and Procedures

Figure 6: *Management control systems package*[15]

Cybernetic controls are about linking behaviors to targets and establishing accountability for variations in performance. Besides, they contain budgets, financial and non-financial measures (p. 292). The CIMA found out that companies mostly concentrate on short-term planning and cybernetic controls (see Brühl & Hanzlick, 2013, p. 10). *Reward and compensation* as a form of control motivate the performance of individuals and groups and thereby links rewards to efforts (p. 293). Planning, cybernetic, and reward and compensation controls are positioned in the middle of the figure, because they are tightly linked to each other in many organizations. *Administrative controls* "direct employee behavior through the organizing of individuals […], the monitoring of behavior and who employees are made accountable to for their behavior […] and through the process of specifying how tasks or behaviors are to be performed" (p. 293). They are at the bottom of the figure, because they build the structure in which the other control types are exercised. Finally, *cultural controls* include "values, beliefs and social norms which are established [to] influence employees behavior" (p. 294). They are at the top of the figure, because they are broad and build the context for the other control types.

3. Legal framework and the relation between risk management and management control systems

First, this chapter presents the legal framework that both RM and MCSs have to comply with, because this is their first similarity. While implementing both, a company has to obey the law and follow several rules. Here, the Committee of Sponsoring Organizations of the Treadway Commission and its famous frameworks are presented. Besides, this chapter introduces the term of corporate governance and the Sarbanes-Oxley Act of 2002. Finally, the main similarities and differences between RM and MCSs are shown.

---

[15] Source: Brown & Malmi, 2008, p. 291.

3.1. Committee of Sponsoring Organizations of the Treadway Commission

The Committee of Sponsoring Organizations of the Treadway Commission (COSO) is a "voluntary private-sector organization dedicated to improving the quality of financial reporting through business ethics, effective internal controls, and corporate governance" (Ong, 2006, p. 392). In 1992 the COSO released *Internal Control – Integrated Framework* with the intention to "enable organizations to [...] develop and maintain systems of internal control that can enhance the likelihood of achieving the entity's objectives and adapt to changes in the business and operating environments" (Landsittel, 2013, p. i). Internal control (IC) is defined here as a process to provide "assurance regarding the achievement of objectives relating to operations, reporting, and compliance" (Landsittel, 2013, p. 3). So it can be said that risk management and management control systems can be seen as parts of the internal control of a company.

In 2001 the COSO developed the *Enterprise Risk Management – Integrated Framework*, which encompasses *Internal Control*, to form a more extensive focus on the broader subject of enterprise risk management (see Flaherty & Maki, 2004, p. v). Enterprise risk management (ERM) is defined as a process "designed to identify potential events that may affect the entity, and manage risk to be within its risk appetite, to provide reasonable assurance regarding the achievement of entity objectives" (Flaherty & Maki, 2004, p. 2). This concept is more similar to the understanding of risk management from pages 2-7 of this paper than to the understanding of management control systems from pages 7-12. The single parts (objectives, components, organizational structure) of both frameworks are presented below in figures 7 and 8.[16]

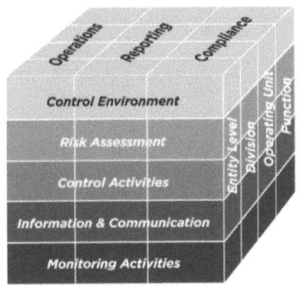
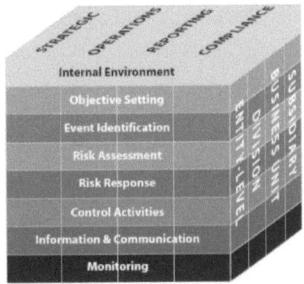

Figure 7: *IC – Integrated Framework*[17]   Figure 8: *ERM – Integrated Framework*[18]

---

[16] For a detailed description of the single parts see: Flaherty & Maki, 2004, pp. 3-6; Landsittel, 2013, pp. 3-7.
[17] Source: Landsittel, 2013, p. 6.
[18] Source: Flaherty & Maki, 2004, p. 5.

3.2. Corporate governance and the Sarbanes-Oxley Act of 2002

There is need to talk about *corporate governance* (CG), because risk management is a key element/task of CG (see Berry et al., 2007, p. 5), and MCSs and CG systems are indivisibly linked (see Merchant & Van der Stede, 2012, p. 553). CG can be seen as the "sets of mechanisms and processes that help ensure that companies are directed [...] to create value for their owners while [...] fulfilling responsibilities to other stakeholders" (Merchant & Van der Stede, 2012, p. 553). Thus, CG contains the mechanisms by which a company is controlled, i.e. rules for the board of directors and audit committees. A board of directors is an elected body of a firm with ultimate decision authority that governs the company and looks after the stakeholders' interests. An audit committee oversees financial reporting, monitors accounting policies, and assures that a company is in compliance with laws. A good CG is important, because it increases trust.

A famous example of legislation for corporate governance is the *Sarbanes-Oxley Act* (SOA/SOX) that – named after its founders – responded to recent corporate financial scandals of companies like *Enron* and *Worldcom* and was passed by the U.S. Congress in 2002. SOX applies to all public companies in the United States (but is also used in enterprises all over the world) and "imposes new and strict guidelines around corporate governance [...] and even imprisonment for senior executives of firms not in compliance" (Levine, 2004, p. 33). The aim of SOX is to "minimize the risk of fraud and significantly misrepresented financial statements" (Best et al., 2006, p. 7), to "improve the transparency, timeliness, and quality of financial reporting" (Merchant & Van der Stede, 2012, p. 555), and so to "restore public confidence in corporate accounting" (Ong, 2006, p. 393). SOX contains many provisions that affect the external auditing industry, the audit committees of the companies' boards of directors and senior company managers.[19]

3.3. The comparison of risk management and management control systems

Now that the legal framework which is important for both risk management and management control systems is worked through, we can compare our findings on risk management from chapter 2.1. to the ones on management control systems from chapter 2.2. I start by listing what both have in common, i.e. similarities, and then I light up the differences. In the end a table shows these findings summarized.

---

[19] The key provisions of SOX can be found in: Merchant & Van der Stede, 2012, pp. 556-557.

3.3.1. The main similarities

3.3.1.1. Objectives

When comparing risk management and management control systems, one recognizes first that in a broader sense both have quite similar goals. Each company has goals that it attempts to achieve in the earlier or later future. A company's management doesn't know what will happen in the future, how employees will behave and whether its objectives will be achieved or not, but both RM and MCSs try to assure future success and livelihood of the firm or to reduce negative impacts and so to support the company in reaching its goals. Both do this in different ways (see chapter 3.3.2.).

3.3.1.2. Strategies

Another similarity concerns a company's strategy, because the reference frame for both risk management and management control systems is the presence of a company-wide strategy. Both educate employees about strategic objectives, i.e. MCSs or PMSs convey "corporate objectives to employees so that they can choose actions consistent with the organizational strategy [and RM] uses internal communication to enlist everyone's participation in the risk management process" (McWhorter et al., 2006, p. 52).

3.3.1.3. Processes

Both risk management and management control systems are no onetime projects, rather processes that should be passed through again and again. Both processes have to be initiated and designed by the concern leadership. The starting point for both is the same and consists of defining and determining objectives, strategies, and threats. Both processes have a quite analogical course. RM begins with the identification of possible risks and threats in the company, and one of the first steps of Ferreira and Otley's PMSs framework is identifying key success factors. Both provide an information basis. When identifying risk areas and key risk factors, one has always to take a look at key success factors/key performance indicators as a kind of warning signs that could be threaten. The next step is assessing risks or – concerning MCSs – measuring performance, so key risk factors and key success factors/performance measures are analyzed and assessed quantitatively/financial or qualitatively/non-financial. Risk treatment is comparable to many parts of MCSs, e.g. defining responsibilities can be seen as a kind of risk avoidance, because when a particular employee has no access to a part of the company, threats can be avoided. Risk reduction for example is comparable to or can be put in place through providing rewards, training, and motivating. I mentioned uncontrollable factors in the chapter about MCSs, for which a company has to purchase insurance. This is a kind of risk transfer. The last process step is risk monitoring that can be compared to Merchant and Van der Stede's cultural controls, because here people monitor each other's behaviors, or to Malmi and Brown's MCS administrative controls which also deal with the monitoring of behavior. All in all it can be said that both RM and MCSs have elements of prevention, detection, and response.

The instruments used in the processes' steps are often the same ones, e.g. key performance indicators for risk assessment and performance measurement, variance analysis to detect differences between results and expected targets for both RM and MCSs, and market measures and accounting measures as warning signs.

The problems occurring due to the use of RM and MCSs do not differ a lot. Both have to think about cost-benefit considerations, because too little investment in control systems and analyzes can lead to existential threats, and too much investment leads to high costs. Another problem is called value orientation which asks whether the concepts should use market measures or accounting measures to measure the entity's value.

3.3.1.4. Balanced scorecards and balanced chance- and risk-cards

In chapter 2.2.1. balanced scorecards (BSCs) were named as examples of management control systems. In general, a BSC transmits the company's visions and strategies into performance measures across the following four perspectives: financial performance, business processes, innovation and knowledge, customer satisfaction. BSCs provide a holistic view of the firm across multiple perspectives, financial and non-financial, thus they help to achieve the company's objectives and strategies (see Beasley et al., 2006, pp. 50-51). Risk management and balanced scorecards have a lot in common, e.g. both "are linked to strategy", "approach strategy by viewing performance measurement and risks", "must be driven from the top of the organization", "focus on individual accountability", and both are ongoing processes (all from Beasley et al., 2006, p. 51). Due to the fact that RM and BSCs have these things in common they can be integrated. Beasley et al. (2006, pp. 54-55) present an integrated balanced scorecard and enterprise risk management framework that links risk management to strategic performance measurement. In doing so, BSCs benefit RM, and RM increases BSCs' effectiveness.

A quite similar idea of balanced scorecards is presented by Diederichs and Kißler (2008, pp. 209-211) and is called *balanced chance- and risk-card* (BCR-card) which provides an integrated view of opportunities and risks. The perspectives that are used can be listed as follows: finances, customer and market, staff, processes, products. For each perspective, risks and opportunities are worked out and then represented with performance indicators that influence the company's value.

3.3.2. The main differences

3.3.2.1. Objectives

The basic goal of risk management and management control systems is the same, namely to help the company to achieve its goals, but upon a closer look it can be said that both do this in different ways, both have different sub objectives. First, human resources have two roles in RM: people as a source of risk and people as risk managers being important in handling risks. It can be said that MCSs focus on human resources risks (e.g. fraud), and RM focuses on all kind of risks that can occur in a company, thus RM analyses internal factors as well as external factors, whereas a MCS only analyses internal factors. A report by Deloitte (2008) says that people and their behavior are often the biggest sources of business risk.

It can be derived from chapters 2.1. and 2.2. that MCSs aim to control behaviors and RM aims to handle risks. While supporting the company, MCSs try to reduce the probability of employees' behavior that could impact the company in a negative way, so it influences people's behavior, and RM tries to avoid, reduce or transfer negative impacts. Thus, RM has broader objectives than MCSs. One can say that RM contains MCS's objectives, but it is not RM's primary target to control employees and to regulate their behavior.

In *A method of Integrating Risk and Performance* by KPMG (2008, p. 7), it is said that enterprise risk management "is focused on defining and mitigating risk, which means moving from higher to lower risk [and performance management] is focused on seeking higher returns on investment, which can often only result from moving from lower to higher risk". This shows that, even RM and MCSs have a lot a in common, they also may conflict. RM and MCSs could stand in the way of each other, because if limitations implemented through RM are too strict, one's performance could be too low.

Another difference concerns the time orientation. An enterprise-wide RM concentrates on strategic, long-term risks, while PMSs draw attention to short-term issues (see Palermo, 2011, p. 4).

3.3.2.2. Processes

In chapter 3.3.1.4. we learned that both risk management and management control systems are driven, designed, and implemented by the top of the company. The concern leadership implements MCSs to control its managers and its heads of department, and managers implement MCSs to control their lower employees. RM tasks are not only taken over by the top management, managers, and heads of departments, but every employee for himself has to make sure that risks are kept at a low level. Thus, RM can also be seen as a part of an employee's performance.

The single process steps are similar to each other (chapter 3.3.1.3.), but of course every system or process, RM or MC, has its own parts that take place and instruments that are used. For example risk takeover is something that one won't find in any way in a MCS, or reward systems are an issue that will never be lit up in a RM system to the extent as in MCSs.

There are two important problems occurring in the processes that differ from each other. The biggest problem during the risk management process is probably the non-observance or the overlook of risks that could lead to enormous damages in the company, and these unidentified or underrated risks represent a major threat. In the management control process the biggest problem consists of myopia, short-term orientation, which for example means that only short-term investments are made even if long-term investments could provide more profit. That is, because incentives and employee's performance measurement are short-term issues.

3.3.3. Summarizing table

In the following I present a table that summarizes all the findings of the chapters above concerning the comparison between risk management and management control systems. This provides a better overview of the similarities and differences.

Subjects/Areas	Similarities	Differences	
		RM	MCS
Legal framework	• while implementing both, one has to obey the law and follow several rules • COSO's Internal control framework contains RM and MCS issues • example of legislation for CG: SOA of 2002	• COSO's ERM framework is more similar to the understanding of RM than to the one of MCSs • RM is a key element/task of CG	• MCSs and CG systems are indivisibly linked

		RM	MCSs
Objectives	• in a broader sense similar goals: assuring future success and livelihood of the firm, reducing negative impacts, and so supporting the company in reaching its goals	• people as a source of risk and people as risk managers in handling risks	• people as a source of risk
		• focus: all kind of risks	• focus: HR risks
		• analyses internal and external factors	• analyses only internal factors
		• aim: to handle risks (to avoid, reduce or transfer negative impacts)	• aim: to control and influence people's behavior
		• RM has broader goals than MCSs	
		• RM contains MCS's objectives, but they are not its primary targets	
		• focus on defining and mitigating risks → moving from higher to lower risk	• focus on seeking higher ROIs → moving from lower to higher risk
		• RM and MCSs may contradict each other	
		• long-term risks/issues	• short-term issues
Strategies	• reference frame for both: presence of a company-wide strategy		
	• both educate employees about strategic objectives		
Processes	• no onetime projects, but rather continuous processes	• every system/process has its own parts that take place (e.g. risk takeover can only be found in RM)	
	• same starting point: defining and determining objectives, strategies, and threats		
	• both have a quite analogical course (see 3.3.1.3.): providing an information basis; measuring risk/ performance; risk treatment strategies have also analogies in MCSs; monitoring		
	• both have elements of prevention, detection, response		
Initiators	• in general, both are driven, designed, and implemented by the top of the company	• RM tasks are taken over by the top management, managers, heads of departments and also by every employee himself (RM as a part of performance)	• concern leadership implements MCSs to control its managers, and managers implement MCSs to control their employees
Instruments	• often the same ones, e.g. key performance indicators, variance analysis, market and accounting measures	• every system/process has its own instruments that are used (e.g. rewards systems are not used to that extent in RM as in MCSs)	
Biggest problems	• necessity for cost-benefit considerations	• non-observance/overlook of risks or unidentified/underrated risks → major threats	• myopia (short-term orientation) leads to a lack of long-term investments
	• value orientation (market or accounting measures)		
Examples of integration	• balanced scorecards		
	• balanced chance- and risk-cards		

Table 1: *Similarities and differences of RM and MCSs – A summary*

4. Summary and conclusion

This paper aimed to present risk management and management control systems and finally to compare them. Risk as the combination of the likelihood of occurrence and the impact of an event is handled by RM, a set of processes/systems, that aim to identify, assess, treat, and monitor risks. MCSs aim to control people's behavior and to direct them in the way of the firm's objectives. Three different frameworks from common literature were presented. The first one dealt with four types of control: results, action, personnel and cultural controls. The second framework considered performance measurement systems, and the third one was about management control systems as a package and described five types of control mechanisms.

The comparison between both showed that RM and MCSs have a lot in common. They have to comply with the same legal frameworks and have in a broader sense the same objectives. Strategies are dealt with in the same way, and the processes that take place have quite similar courses. The initiators are mostly the same, and some instruments can be used for both. Nevertheless the differences should not be ignored. On closer inspection they have different sub objectives and may also contradict each other, and every system has also its own instruments and process parts.

Thus, concerning the question which one of both is more efficient and effective in supporting the company it cannot be said that one of them is better, because each one helps the company to reach its goals and to accomplish its strategies in its own way, and businesses cannot waive one of the two. Both are necessary, because RM does not light up HR risks and behavioral issues to the extent as MCSs do, and MCSs never consider other threats than misconducts. RM and MCSs may help each other, because if a company-wide risk understanding and awareness is introduced by RM, employees become conscious of what are risky activities and may not behave against the company's aims.

Therefore, one solution could be to integrate or link both RM and MCSs like in this paper's example of balanced scorecards and balanced chance- and risk-cards. A research article by McWorther et al. (2006, pp. 51-55) shows that PMSs improve RM, and so further research questions can be the following ones: How can RM and MCSs be integrated or linked to improve each other? What kind of frameworks can be thought of? Some literature provides good starting points for this further research.[20] They consider possibilities how to integrate risk and performance.

---

[20] For example see: Apanaschik et al., 2009, pp. 1-28; Boicova & Slagmulder, 2012, pp. 1-9; Economist Intelligence Unit, 2010, pp. 1-14; KPMG, 2008, pp. 1-15; Palermo, 2011, pp. 1-7.

List of references

Abernethy, M. A., & Chua, W. F. (1996). Field study of control system 'Redesign': the impact of institutional process on strategic choice. *Contemporary Accounting Research, 13*(2), 569–606.

Apanaschik, G., Atkinson, J., & Pittman, D. (2009). *Seizing opportunity: Linking risk and performance.* US: PricewaterhouseCoopers.

Beasley, M. S., Chen, A., Nunez, K., & Wright, L. (2006). WORKING Hand IN Hand: Balanced Scorecards AND Enterprise Risk Management. *Strategic Finance, 87*(9), 49–55.

Berry, A. J., Burke, G. T., & Collier, P. M. (2007). *Risk and management accounting: Best practice guidelines for enterprise-wide internal control procedures.* Oxford: CIMA.

Best, P., Green, P., Rikhardsson, P., & Rosemann, M. (2006). *Business Process Risk Management, Compliance and Internal Control: A Research Agenda.* Department of Business Studies, Management Accounting Research Group, Aarhus School of Business.

Boicova, M. & Slagmulder, R. (2012). *Integrating risk into performance: Reporting to the board of directors.* London: CIMA.

Brown, D. A., & Malmi, T. (2008). Management control systems as a package: opportunities, challenges and research directions. *Management accounting research, 19*(4), 287–300.

Brühl, R. & Hanzlick, M. (2013). *Management Control Systems as a Package: Preliminary findings in Germany.* London: CIMA

Chartered Institute of Management Accountants. (2005). *Official terminology.* Oxford: CIMA.

Cottin, C., & Döhler, S. (2013). *Risikoanalyse: Modellierung, Beurteilung und Management von Risiken mit Praxisbeispielen* (2., überarb. u. erw. Aufl. 2013). *Studienbücher Wirtschaftsmathematik.* Wiesbaden: Springer.

Deloitte. (2008). *Taking the reins: HR's opportunity to play a leadership role in governance, risk management, and compliance.* Retrieved from http://www.deloitte.com/assets/Dcom-UnitedStates/Local%20Assets/Documents/us_consulting_Takingthe Reins_091911.pdf (Access 15.12.2013)

Diederichs, M. (2012). *Risikomanagement und Risikocontrolling* (3., vollst. überarb. Aufl). *Finance competence.* München: Vahlen.

Diederichs, M., & Kißler, M. (2008). *Aufsichtsratreporting: Corporate Governance, Compliance und Controlling.* München: Vahlen.

Doody, H. (2009). *Fraud risk management: A guide to good practice.* London: CIMA.

Economist Intelligence Unit. (2010). *Integrating risk and performance: Collaborating for better decisions and greater buy-in.* UK: The Economist.

Ferreira, A., & Otley, D. (2009). The design and use of performance management systems: An extended framework for analysis. *Management accounting research, 20*(4), 263–282.

Flaherty, J. J., & Maki, T. (2004). *Enterprise risk management - integrated framework: Executive summary.* New York: COSO.

Frenkel, M., Hommel, U., & Rudolf, M. (2000). *Risk management: Challenge and opportunity*. Berlin, Heidelberg: Springer.

Gleißner, W. (2011). *Grundlagen des Risikomanagements im Unternehmen: Controlling, Unrternehmensstrategie und wertorientiertes Management* (2., komplett überarb. und erw. Aufl). München: Vahlen.

Institute of Risk Management. (2002). *A Risk Management Standard*. London: IRM.

Kajüter, P. (2012). *Risikomanagement im Konzern: Eine empirische Analyse börsennotierter Aktienkonzerne*. München: Vahlen.

Kerr, S. (2004). Establishing organizational goals and rewards. *Academy Of Management Executive, 18*(4), 122–123.

KPMG. (2008). *A Method of Integrating Risk and Performance*. Retrieved from http://www.kpmg.com/Global/en/IssuesAndInsights/ArticlesPublications/Pages/A-method-of-integrating-risk-and-performance.aspx (Access 15.12.2013)

Landsittel, D. L. (2013). *Internal control - integrated framework: Executive summary*. Durham, NC: American Institute of Certified Public Accountants.

Levine, R. (2004). Risk management systems: Understanding the need. *Information Systems Management, 21*(2), 31–37.

Malmi, T., & Schäffer, U. (2013). Management control systems in day-to-day business. *Controlling & management review: Zeitschrift für Controlling & Management, 57*(5), 40–45.

McWhorter, L. B., Matherly, M., & Frizzell, D. M. (2006). The Connection between PERFORMANCE MEASUREMENT and RISK MANAGEMENT. *Strategic Finance, 87*(8), 50–55.

Merchant, K. A., & Van der Stede, Wim A. (2012). *Management control systems: Performance measurement, evaluation and incentives* (3. ed). Harlow: Financial Times Prentice Hall.

Meyer, M., Robbins, M., & Roodt, G. (2011). Human resources risk management: Governing people risks for improved performance. *SA journal of human resource management: SAJHRM, 9*(1), 310–321.

Nevries, P., & Strauß, E. (2008). Aufgaben des Controllings im Rahmen des Risikomanagementprozesses: Eine empirische Untersuchung in deutschen Großkonzernen. *Controlling & Management: ZfCM; Zeitschrift für Controlling und Management, 52*(2), 106–111.

Oehler, A., & Unser, M. (2002). *Finanzwirtschaftliches Risikomanagement* (2., verb. Aufl). Berlin: Springer.

Ong, M. K. (2006). *Risk management: A modern perspective*. Burlington, MA: Academic Press/Elsevier.

Palermo, T. (2011). *Integrating risk and performance in management reporting. Research executive summary series: v. 8, issue 1*. London: CIMA.

Porter, M. E. (1999). *Wettbewerbsvorteile: Spitzenleistungen erreichen und behaupten* (5., durchges. und erw. Aufl). Frankfurt/Main: Campus-Verl.

Romeike, F. (2002). Risikomanagement als Grundlage einer wertorientierten Unternehmenssteuerung. *Controlling in Consultingunternehmen: Instrumente, Konzepte, Perspektiven* (pp. 245-262). Wiesbaden: Gabler.

Romeike, F. (2005). *Modernes Risikomanagement: Die Markt-, Kredit- und operationellen Risiken zukunftsorientiert steuern*. Weinheim: Wiley-VCH.

Spellmann, F., & Unser, M. (1998). Zinsänderungsrisiko und Bonitätsänderungsrisiko integriert betrachtet: Ein Überblick über den Stand der Literatur. *Credit Risk und Value-at-Risk Alternativen: Herausforderungen für das Risk-Management* (pp. 259-280). Stuttgart: Schäffer-Poeschel.

Tirole, J. (2001). Corporate governance. *Econometrica, 69*(1), 1–35.

Wall, F. (2003). Kompatibilität des betriebswirtschaftlichen Risikomanagement mit den gesetzlichen Anforderungen: Eine Analyse mit Blick auf die Abschlussprüfung. *Die Wirtschaftsprüfung, 56*(9), 457–471.